Did JESUS really exist?

and 51 other questions

Nikolaas Sintobin SJ

Published by Messenger Publications, 2020

First published by KokBoekencentrul, Utrecht, Netherlands
www.kokboekencentrum.nl

ISBN 978 1 78812 121 7

Book Design: Andries Mol
Artwork: Messenger Publications
Illustrations: Paris Selinas
Author Photograph: Jaco Klamer

Typeset in Minion Pro and Skirt
Printed by Hussar Books

Messenger Publications,
37 Lower Leeson Street, Dublin D02 W938
www.messenger.ie

Introduction

What do Christians believe? What is typical of Christian faith and of how Christians live out their faith?

With fifty-two questions and answers, this book gives you an overview of the Christian faith. You can read it as an introduction to Christianity. If you are already familiar with Christianity, then this book is a deepening refresher course on the basic elements.

The questions are taken from life: is faith for simple souls? Did Jesus really exist? What do people do in heaven? Is God a judge who condemns? Why should you forgive yourself? Does suffering make sense? Are the other religions wrong? Has Jesus laughed?

Each answer takes a maximum of two minutes to read. The answer is always followed by two questions to work on individually or together with others. There are also references to five other questions relating to the subject under discussion. At the end of the book is a list with a short description of fifty-two common words such as prayer, grace, heaven, Easter, sin, sacrament and devil. In the text these words are marked with an asterisk.

Enjoy your reading!

Nikolaas Sintobin SJ

Contents

Foreword

Think about some of the questions you always wanted to ask about the Christian faith, about Catholicism, about God, about Jesus, about the Church. In this book you will find many such questions put in a simple way and responded to in a manner that is fresh and easy to read. Yes, you will find much more detail presented in a scholarly manner in the *Catechism of the Catholic Church* (1994) but here Nikolaas Sintobin SJ uses a conversational tone to open up the questions of faith that really matter – but often lie deep within us and unspoken.

It is interesting that in our times, when so much is available on the internet and people's beliefs and attitudes are commented on forcefully on social media, we can still lack clarity about the central tenets of the Christian faith and the hope-filled life and spirituality it can give rise to. This little book is invaluable in bringing together fifty-two interesting questions fundamental for Catholics to grapple with, integrating their faith with life. Holding these questions together in one place, this volume helps us to make sense of who Jesus is for us and how he has helped us understand God, as well as who we are called to be. Lots of misunderstandings are dispelled for us too. Science and religion can work well together. Reincarnation is incompatible with the Christian belief in the resurrection. The Bible, the Word of God, contains many different types of texts which cannot all be read in the same manner.

There are so many ways in which this small treasure chest can be used. Pick it up yourself once a week for each of the 52 weeks in a year and reflect on one of the questions – or look for a question and a response you are particularly interested in – or read it through from beginning to end. Whatever way you go about it you can keep coming back.

Certainly teachers of Religious Education can have this summary of key questions to hand and use it to support their work in schools. Catechists working in parishes, with adults as well as with young people, will find it a helpful starting point for discussion. It could also be used as the focus for a conversation among family and friends, with a parish book club or with a prayer group.

The story that is opened up for us here is a meditation on the whole of life and on our relationship with God. It uncovers for us the mystery of God and the mystery of humanity too. Perhaps this is the moment to look further and deeper into Christian faith as well as into the many ways in which the Christian life can be lived well today.

Dr Gareth Byrne

Director, Mater Dei Centre for Catholic Education

QUESTION 1

Is believing exceptional?

Every human being believes, for believing is actually just as normal as eating, drinking and breathing. Think of a little child who learns to ride a bike. The child firmly believes that their father or mother will intervene immediately if something goes wrong. Think of a young man who is going to marry his girlfriend. He can never be one hundred per cent sure that she really wants to live with him all his life. He dares to take on this adventure anyway because he believes in it. He trusts her. It is certainly no coincidence that both Latin and Greek – two languages that are important in the history of the Christian faith – use the same word for trust and faith.

Complete certainty *is* exceptional. There are always things you do not know, and that require you to take a leap into the unknown. Often you do this with your eyes closed, more often you don't even realise that you are jumping. Trusting in others is essential to being human. From day one in this world, life teaches you that you have to trust others to get on.

When it comes to believing in God*, things get a bit more complicated. The child who learns to cycle sees and feels that their father or mother is close. You cannot see God, and that makes the jump into the unknown a lot bigger.

Maybe you've heard people say, 'I wish I could believe in God'. Believing is not something you can just decide on. It takes more than that. Believing in God – but also trusting people – is something you have to experience over and over again.

- Do you find believing easy or difficult?

- Have you noticed any change in this over the years?

See also questions 2, 6, 26, 49, 52.

QUESTION 2

Is faith for simple souls?

Faith is for all souls, simple or otherwise. People with little study or education behind them can be profoundly religious, or not religious at all. Young children can have an amazing life of faith, or not. Quite a few political leaders and successful entrepreneurs are convinced Christians while others are not. There are those who, by studying, discover their faith while others find themselves losing their faith in God* during their time as students.

Faith is not about knowing or not knowing, or about greater or lesser intelligence. Yet, Christians do not believe in just anything. That is why it is important to try to understand what faith is about. It is normal that children are taught languages, mathematics, history and many other subjects at school. Many people study such subjects for a long time. In the same way there is a lot of knowledge to be gained about the Christian faith, some of it requiring study. The study of Christian faith often results in enlightening and important insights about life.

However, many people's knowledge of the Christian faith does not go much further than a few generalities and prejudices. Some hardly know anything about it. They know Christmas is about the baby Jesus* and Good Friday is about his death, and Pentecost*, but are confused about their meaning. Without some

knowledge it is not surprising that for many everything that has to do with Christianity seems unbelievable, and at most good for simple souls. Unknown indeed often makes unloved.

- Do you think it's important to increase your knowledge of religion?

- What or who helped you to know more about your faith?

See also questions 1, 14, 30, 42, 49.

QUESTION 3

Can you be a Christian and yet doubt your faith?

Doubt is part of the Christian faith. Believing is not the same as knowing. When your stomach rumbles, you know that you are hungry. You also know that this hunger will stop when you eat. People want certainty. What you know, you can control. People like that. It gives them a sense of security. With God*, that doesn't work. Believing in God and in the risen Jesus* is believing in something and someone you can't reach with your common sense. The mystery of God is reached in the mind and heart.

You can believe with your heart and soul that God exists and that Jesus lives. That doesn't mean that doubt can't strike. Is it all true? Don't I confuse my dreams with reality? This can hurt. Don't worry too much about it. Doubt comes, doubt goes.

A special example of doubt in faith can be seen in the stories of the apparitions*, at the end of the Gospels*. They describe encounters between the risen Jesus and his friends. In almost all these stories, doubt plays an important role. They can hardly believe that the man who died on a cross is alive again, and that they can see, hear and touch Jesus. Some even eat with him. If there was any doubt among those first believers, then it is normal that Christians today sometimes doubt that the whole story is true.

Doubt also has good sides. It prevents you from believing on autopilot. It can be an incentive to pay more attention to your life of faith and to keep looking for the core of it.

- Do you sometimes doubt? Which beliefs in particular?

- How do you deal with this doubt? What helps you with it?

See also questions 1, 4, 19, 46, 48.

QUESTION 4

Can a believer be critical?

Believing has nothing to do with 'gazing at the sky and letting your mind go blank'. Faith and a critical attitude go hand in hand. Faith is about God* and therefore about life's deepest mystery. Believers wants to entrust themselves to this mystery, even if it sometimes goes beyond their understanding. At the same time it is necessary to purify faith from superstition and therefore from unbelief. That is why Christians find it important to understand the Christian faith as much as possible with their mind, knowing that the starting point of Christianity* – the resurrection* of Jesus* – completely escapes the laws of nature and human logic. However important the critical mind may be, it does not have the last word for the believer.

The critical attitude has an important pitfall: suspicion. It is important to recognise this pitfall because it can kill trust. Without trust there is no faith. Therefore moderation is important, including with regard to the desire to understand; a desire that in itself is good. You better not wait for the moment when you understand everything with your mind, before you can believe. That is simply not possible.

Faith in God is not about sorcery or fairy tales. Just look at the harshness of the life and death of Jesus. Yet experience shows that people sometimes use faith as a shield against life, quietly hoping

that God, as a wizard-figure, will solve all their problems. It is important to remember this is not how it happened in the life of Jesus. Yet, in the name of faith, strange things are still being said and done today, sometimes with the best of intentions, sometimes with less grand intentions. That is why critical thinking is so important. The critical eye can unmask the weeds in the garden of our faith.

- Do you deal critically with what you believe or do not believe?

- Have you ever weeded your garden of faith?

See also questions 2, 5, 6, 26, 48.

QUESTION 5

Can faith and science get along?

Faith and science are not mutually exclusive. They are not competitors. The reason is simple. Faith and science answer different questions. It is therefore not surprising that among great scientists you find both believers and non-believers. The inventor of the theory of the Big Bang, Georges Lemaître, was a learned professor and a Catholic* priest*.

Faith gives an answer to questions like: why do we exist? What is the meaning of life? Why is there something instead of nothing? Nuclear physics, chemistry or mathematics can't answer those questions. That is not their domain. The question the scientist wants to answer is *how* our world works. For centuries people thought and believed that they could find the answer to that question in the Bible*. It has only been a few centuries since Christians started to disassemble these questions, an unravelling that is still going on.

Many people say that they believed as a child, but that they lost their faith when they discovered science. One of the reasons for this is that many people's knowledge of faith has been limited to the knowledge they had of it when they were children. It is not surprising that such a belief is undermined by the confrontation with scientific thinking. For others, it is precisely the practice of science that is the starting point of a path of faith: who or what is at the origin of this incredibly beautiful cosmos?

- Do you think there is a contradiction between faith and science?

- Does science influence what you believe?

See also questions 1, 2, 4, 8, 17.

QUESTION 6

Are you born a Christian?

Being a Christian is not congenital or hereditary, but of course you get a lot from your parents. Your family has a big influence on who you are and who you become. This also applies to what you believe. Yet, the Christian faith is not just passed on from parent to child.

You don't choose your mother tongue, you receive it. That doesn't mean that you can't learn other languages later on, but the language in which you grow up always retains something unique and definite. You can't leave it behind you. For faith, it's different. If you grow up in a Christian family, you can stop believing. The other way around is also possible: you were born in an unbelieving or non-believing environment, but one day you start believing in Jesus*.

Education and environment are important, but in the end being a Christian is the result of a personal choice. You become a Christian. Even if you have been brought up in the Christian faith, sooner or later you have to go for it yourself. Someone else cannot decide this in your place. Christian faith and freedom* go hand in hand.

The personal choice, however important, is not enough. Some would like to believe. They do everything they can to believe. Yet,

they find that they don't have the faith. At the end of the day, faith is something you receive. It is offered to you and then you can say 'yes' or 'no' to it. Christians call this mystery the grace* of faith.

- How and when did you come to your faith?

- Which people, experiences and events are or have been important in your faith story?

See also questions 1, 14, 47, 49, 50.

QUESTION 7

Can a human being meet God?

Every human being can meet God*. This happens all the time, even though most people are unaware of it. Christians believe that experiencing deep joy has to do with experiencing God's presence. This is especially true for joy that leaves a good aftertaste following the event that caused the joy. You can experience that joy while praying* or in the church* but just as well at work, in the kitchen, in a museum or walking in nature. That joy can be strong. It is often quiet and almost unnoticeable. Joy that continues to resonate says something about where and how God is present in a person's life.

Some people have a special gift for experiencing God's presence, a gift so strong that they describe that experience as a union with God. This union can be both physical and emotional, and is always unexpected. Such a person is called a mystic. These mystics can be found in all major religions, but especially in Christianity*. Typically, these people are very discreet about it. It is so intimate that they prefer to keep it to themselves. There are few people to whom this is given.

- Being close, or more distant from God, what does that mean for you?

- Have you ever had an experience that you would describe as an encounter with God?

See also questions 21, 23, 25, 45, 46.

QUESTION 8

Did God create the world in seven days?

The biblical story of creation* is a true story. However, it is not a scientific report on how and when God* created the world. It is a different kind of truth. You don't have to take the creation story *literally*.

The Bible* begins with the story of creation. It dates from about 500 BCE: the period of the return of the Jews* to Israel, after they were exiled to Babylon. Israel was promised by God to the Jewish people, and they were forced to leave that country. This led to a great crisis of faith and doubt: how can a God who loves allow this? But then they are able to return and the Jews will definitely believe that God loves people through thick and thin. God keeps liberating and forgiving them.

In Babylon, where the Jews lived for fifty years, creation stories were common. Once back in Israel, the Jews, as a sign of their gratitude and joy, wrote their 'own' creation story. But this was a very different kind of creation story than was usual in Babylon. There the stories were about a violent struggle between several gods, in which the bad god overcomes, and the human being is no more than a slave. In the biblical story of creation God emerges as a good and faithful God. Humanity is the crown jewel of creation.

In summary, one can say that the biblical story of creation has its origin in a real experience of the people of Israel, but if you read it as a press release about how God created the world in seven days, you are wrong. It poetically expresses the belief that the Jewish people – and more broadly, humans – owe their existence to the faithful love of God. The writer uses a form that fits his time: a story of creation.

Who or what do you think is at the origin of the world?

Do you believe that God loves you?

See also questions 9, 10, 14, 40, 43.

QUESTION 9

What did God do before he created the world?

Before God* created the world, he did what he has always done and will do: he loved. After all, God is love. Everything God does or does not do has to do with love. People like to ask the question about the before and the after. As far as God is concerned, this question is somewhat problematic. Before God created the world there was no time, and if there is no time, there can be no before and after. Only eternity. Time has only come through creation*. From then on the sequence of events began: past, present and future. So time itself was also created by God.

God is love and when God creates, it means that he no longer wants to keep that love for himself, but wants to share his love with something or someone. It is part of God's being that God creates, because true love reaches beyond itself. God has no choice but to create with love that is overflowing. That is why God's creation is not something one-off. Something from long ago. No, God creates constantly. If God would cease to create for just one moment, everything that is would immediately stop existing. The whole creation exists and continues to exist thanks to God's creative power of love.

- God is love. What does that mean to you?
- Do you believe that God constantly creates and gives life to everything that exists?

See also questions 8, 10, 22, 26, 37.

QUESTION 10

Is God a man or a woman?

No, God* is not a man. He is not a woman either. Being a man or a woman is about sexuality and procreation. God transcends the distinction between man and woman. Thus there is no point talking about the gender of God.

Yet Jesus* speaks of his Father*. He invites his disciples – and thus also Christians – to pray to God* as 'our Father'. Even before Jesus, the Bible* called God 'Father'. It is an expression of God's tender love. But in the Bible, God is also compared to a mother who loves her infant. Jesus also compares the care and love of God in different places with that of a woman. A lot of people are happy with that, because for some people it is difficult to use the word 'father' when they talk about God.

It is normal to describe God and his attitude towards people with human images about love, giving life, being faithful, protecting. These human images have the advantage that they are appealing and familiar. At the same time they are limited and imperfect. Fortunately God is more than these images.

❧ What words, images or gestures do you use when you speak to God?

- Do you find the word 'Father' meaningfully expresses your relationship with God?

See also questions 8, 9, 15, 45, 26.

QUESTION 11

Can you be a Christian without believing in Jesus?

Without faith in Jesus* you cannot call yourself a Christian. Christians believe in God*, but so do Jews* and Muslims. Believers of these religions pray* and express their faith in rituals. An outsider sometimes doesn't see much difference between all the ways of praying and celebrating. The values and norms of Christians do not differ much from those of other religions. What does distinguish Christians from all other religions is their faith in Jesus Christ*. Hence the name 'Christian'.

Christians believe that Jesus was the best person who ever lived, but they believe even more than that about him. In particular, that Jesus was completely human and at the same time completely God. That in him God has become man and a man has become God. This means that Christians believe that by getting to know Jesus, you can discover who God is. Also that a person, by trying to live like Jesus, can come closer to God and so live life as it was meant to be.

Christians also believe that Jesus rose after his death. That he lives again. They don't believe in a dead body, but in a living person with whom you can have a relationship. The intensity of that relationship varies from person to person, and can also vary throughout a person's life. One will talk about friendship with Jesus, another about a love affair. That relationship sometimes feels strong. At other times it may seem weak, almost dormant, even though you might have wanted it to be different.

- What importance do you attach to the person of Jesus?

- Can you imagine believing that Jesus is still alive today?

See also questions 7, 12, 14, 45, 52.

QUESTION 12

Did Jesus really exist?

Whether Jesus* really existed is not really an open question. There are enough historical sources that show that Jesus existed. The most important is the New Testament*, the second part of the Bible*. This is a collection of books and letters from the first century of our era. It contains a lot of historical information about Jesus. In addition, writings of Jewish and Roman historians from the second half of the first century and from the beginning of the second century tell about Jesus and Christians. Finally, there are the results of archaeological research. These sources prove that Jesus existed. Most historians agree that he was born between 6 and 4 BCE and died in the year 30 CE.

The fact that Jesus actually lived, died on a cross and then rose from the dead, is of great importance for the Christian faith. For Christians, this means that God* has shared our human life, down to the smallest details, up to and including death. The infinitely great God did not only create the humans. He went to live in the body and spirit of a human person. God has become equal to humanity. If you think about it, it seems totally unlikely, but it is the core of the Christian faith.

Some other religions look differently at the question of whether the stories about their own heroes really happened. In Hinduism, for

example, there are all kinds of wonderful stories about the gods. Whether they actually happened is not so important for a Hindu.

- Do you believe that Jesus really existed?

- If you were to meet Jesus now, is there something you would like to ask or say to him?

See also questions 11, 14, 15, 43, 50.

QUESTION 13

What is the importance of the hidden life of Jesus?

The Gospels* tell little about the birth of Jesus* and much about his public life, at the end of his short existence. We hardly know anything about the period in between. These years in the life of Jesus are called his 'hidden life'. Evangelist Luke summarises this long period as follows, 'Jesus grew up, and he became wiser and wiser. God* loved Him, and so did many' (Lk 2:52).

It is usually assumed that Jesus spent that time in Nazareth, a small village in Galilee, a province with little prestige. He probably lived there with his parents. According to tradition he worked as a carpenter, just like Joseph*, his father.

Was Jesus' great project in storage all this time? Wasn't he yet fully the Son of God during those years? Can something be learned from those thirty years or did so little happen in that period that there is actually nothing to tell about?

Christians believe that during his 'hidden life' Jesus was already Son of God and therefore completely God. In the period in which he grew as a human being from child to adolescent, and from young adult to an adult man Jesus was completely God. Christians think this is important. It means that an ordinary, unobtrusive life

– about which there is little to tell – is so important to God that God, for many years, wanted to experience it. The most famous man in history was completely unknown for most of his life. In other words: even a simple, unknown life in all humility is valuable. It can be a divine life.

- How do you imagine the hidden life of Jesus?

- Do you know inconspicuous people in whose lives you believe that God is really at work?

See also questions 11, 12, 15, 31, 52.

QUESTION 14

What is the message of Jesus?

Jesus* has a joyful message of prosperity, hope and happiness. In a single word, his message is called 'Gospel'*. That literally means 'Good News'. You can find that message in the four Gospels, written by Matthew, Mark, Luke and John. Each of them, in their own way, tells the story of Jesus.

The content of that message is that God* wants to offer everyone the opportunity to live in freedom*, peace, justice and love. That message has everything to do with the person of Jesus himself. Jesus is like the door that gives access to full communion with God. From the beginning of his action, Jesus calls upon people to believe in this Good News. The life of Jesus is the start of the definitive realisation of that bond between God and humanity. No other person than Jesus has ever claimed this about himself: 'I am the way, the truth and the life' (Jn 14:6).

The Good News of Jesus is not a task that you carry out alone. No one is capable of that. Rather, it is the promise that God is fully committed to this. Jesus asks the people to cooperate.

The Gospel is never fully realised on earth. That will only happen in life after death. The more a person already cooperates with this, the more he or she can participate in this perfect joy in heaven*.

The message of Jesus is addressed to all people, without distinction. It is addressed particularly to the excluded and the poor. Jesus says about them that they are the first to have access to this full communion with God. Just like small children who can easily entrust themselves entirely to the care and love of their parents.

- What about the message of Jesus appeals most to you?

- Are there aspects of the Gospel that are difficult for you to deal with?

See also questions 12, 15, 22, 49, 52,

QUESITON 15

Is Jesus God or human?

Christians believe that Jesus* is all God* and at the same time all human. Not a kind of mixture with part divine and part human qualities. Jesus is one hundred per cent human and one hundred per cent God. Not two personalities in one body, but a unique person who has both a divine and a human nature. Both natures are equally important. In Jesus, God is humanised and humanity is deified. This is so difficult to understand with the mind that it took more than 400 years for Christians to be able to put it into words somewhat well.

Christians believe that Jesus is the Son of God. This means that he is so similar to God, that he himself is God. By his birth from Mary* Jesus has not ceased to be God. From his conception he was God, and he has remained so to this day.

When you see old paintings of the baby Jesus in a museum, it is striking that his private parts are often depicted in detail. In other paintings you can see how the child Jesus eagerly sucks on the breast of Mary, his mother. This is no coincidence. This was done deliberately to make it clear that Jesus was not just pretending to be human, but that he really was. With all that this means, with our normal human needs. In Jesus God became human and lived completely as a human person.

Jesus shows that being human and being God can go together. Through him, being human has been given a divine rank. This means that you in turn can become like God, when you live like Jesus. Does that sound unbelievable? Yet it belongs to the core of Christianity*.

- Do you see something divine in the person, the life and the message of Jesus?

- By living like Jesus, people can in turn become like God. Does this speak to you?

See also questions 12, 16, 19, 20, 22.

QUESTION 16

Is Mary a virgin?

When Jesus* was still on this earth, many people believed that He was different from others. There was a special authority emanating from Him. He acted and spoke as no one had ever done. After his death and resurrection* people quickly started asking questions about who Jesus really was and how you could explain his otherness. They began to think about his origins. At that time it started with the question 'Who really is his Father*?' Was his father an ordinary man? Surely that is not possible! A man of whom it is believed that he is God's Son* cannot be the fruit of the sexual intercourse between a man and a woman.

Belief in the divinity of Jesus explains why Christians call Mary* a virgin. The virginity of Mary is not so much a claim about Mary, but about Jesus. This religious expression is a special way of saying that the actual Father of Jesus is none other than God himself.

In the Bible* this special event is expressed by Gabriel, an angel*. Gabriel visits Mary before she becomes pregnant. He says, 'The Holy Spirit* will come to you. And by the power of the Most High God, you will become pregnant. Therefore, your child will belong to God, and he will be called the son of God' (Lk 1:15). This explains why Jesus spoke in a special way about God and also to God. He did not just call him, reverently, 'Father', like the other believing

Jews*. Jesus addressed God with 'Dad', a pet name. Something that was unheard of at the time.

- What does the belief that God is the Father of every human being mean to you?

- Do you believe that Jesus had a unique bond with God?

See also questions 12, 15, 17, 26, 32.

QUESTION 17

Did Jesus do miracles?

Christians believe that Jesus* worked miracles*. For example, the Gospels* describe numerous healings of the sick by Jesus. However, Jesus is not a magician who conjures up rabbits from his hat. His miracles are not tricks that he performed to impress. But what then?

In the time of Jesus, everyone believed in miracles. There was no understanding of the laws of nature. Thunder and lightning, for example, were taken as signs of God's anger and not an easily explained natural phenomenon. Everything that happened in the world was directly attributed to God's intervention. What was unusual was called a miracle. This is no longer the case for us today.

Is a miracle, then, something that modern science cannot explain? Again, this is not enough to explain one. Science is not perfect. There are still many things that cannot be explained. Yet these are not all miracles. In other words, it is not science that can decide whether something is miraculous or not. But on what does it depend?

There is something special about the miracles of Jesus. Sometimes he manages to perform a miracle immediately, but there are also cases where he has to start again. Sometimes it doesn't work at all.

The reason for the latter is people's unbelief. Here is the heart of the matter. The miracles of Jesus ultimately have to do with faith in God. A miracle is a special sign in which the believer sees God's goodness and care for us at work. Whether it is about a healing or a special natural phenomenon, it is ultimately the faith that makes that you can see a certain event as a sign of the greatness and the goodness of God. That is why Jesus, after a miracle, says several times 'Your faith has saved you' (Mk 5:34).

- Are there miracles of Jesus that particularly appeal to you?

- Do these miracles teach you something about Jesus and about his message?

See also questions 4, 5, 6, 14, 22.

QUESTION 18

Did God want Jesus to be crucified?

People decided to crucify Jesus*. This was not God's desire. Crucifixion* was the most humiliating, painful and shameful execution there was, and extremely painful too. If God had wanted this for his Son, you could only draw one conclusion: he is a perverse God.

Yet the cross has become the pre-eminent symbol of the Christian faith. It took a few centuries for this to happen, so tremendous was the horror and repugnance of the first generations of Christians against this terrible torture. Gradually believers began to see the cross as the place where it became clear how unimaginably great God's love for humanity is. God wanted Jesus to bear witness to this love.

Jesus could have avoided his death on the cross. It was his conscious choice not to flee from suffering. He wanted to pass on God's love in words and especially in deeds, to the extreme. Even though he seemed to get nothing in return. Even though he was abandoned by everyone. Even though it hurt terribly. Even if love would cost him his life. No evil or injustice could stop Jesus. Even on the cross he continued to love people and forgive them, so strong was the love that he himself experienced from God whom he called his Father*.

- What do you think about Jesus' death on the cross?
- Have you experienced anything like a cross experience in your own life? How did you deal with that?

See also questions 14, 22, 34, 38, 39.

QUESTION 19

Has Jesus risen from the dead?

The Gospels* do not describe Jesus' resurrection* at Easter* anywhere. What you can read is that he became alive again after his death. It is not known exactly how this happened. The grave is empty, the witnesses say. They also say that they have seen, heard and touched him. Some even ate with him. Their encounters are real; Jesus is not a ghost that lights up. Yet there is a lot of mystery around it. The risen Jesus comes in while the doors are closed. Another time he disappears inexplicably. More than once he comes to his disciples, but 'they don't recognise him' (Lk 24:16).

The resurrection of Jesus means that he has entered the world of God*, a world that is still unimaginable for us. Jesus' resurrection does not mean that his dead body began to breathe and move again. He has not become an ordinary, living and therefore mortal man again. The risen Jesus is immortal. He is different and yet the same.

It is not easy to believe in the resurrection. It is no coincidence that in almost all apparitions* there is unbelief and doubt, also among the people who knew Jesus very well. At the same time these hesitant witnesses are going to proclaim his resurrection.

Perhaps this is the strongest proof of the reality of the resurrection.

The disciples of Jesus were traumatised by the shameful failure that Jesus' (and their own) life's work had turned out to be. They had fled in all directions. Shortly after that the same people are going to proclaim with unimaginable passion that their hero is the Saviour of the people. They no longer conceal his death on the cross. They will now proclaim it almost with pride. Between both moments they must have experienced something even more shocking and dramatic than the catastrophe of Jesus' crucifixion: his resurrection.

- What do you think the resurrection of Jesus means?

- Do you relate to any of the doubts of the first witnesses of the resurrection?

See also questions 3, 14, 22, 27, 51.

QUESTION 20

Does it matter if Jesus has risen?

The apostle* Paul* speaks bluntly. In one of his letters he writes, 'If Christ* has not risen, then all we say is nonsense. Then the whole faith is meaningless' (1 Cor 15:14). Without resurrection* there is no question of Christianity*. Without faith in the resurrection of Jesus* there is no Christian faith. If Jesus has not been resurrected, then at best his life is an impressive story with a tragic ending: his execution.

Jesus did not raise himself from the dead. It was God* who did so. At the end of the life and death of Jesus, this is the personal signature of God. By doing so, He confirms and approves what Jesus thought was important. Through the resurrection it becomes clear that the story of Jesus, the Son of God is the story of God.

Because of the resurrection it is clear to Christians that Jesus' Good News really comes from God. Jesus is the example that every person can follow. His way of love is the God-approved way that leads people to life as God intended.

Do you believe that Jesus has risen?

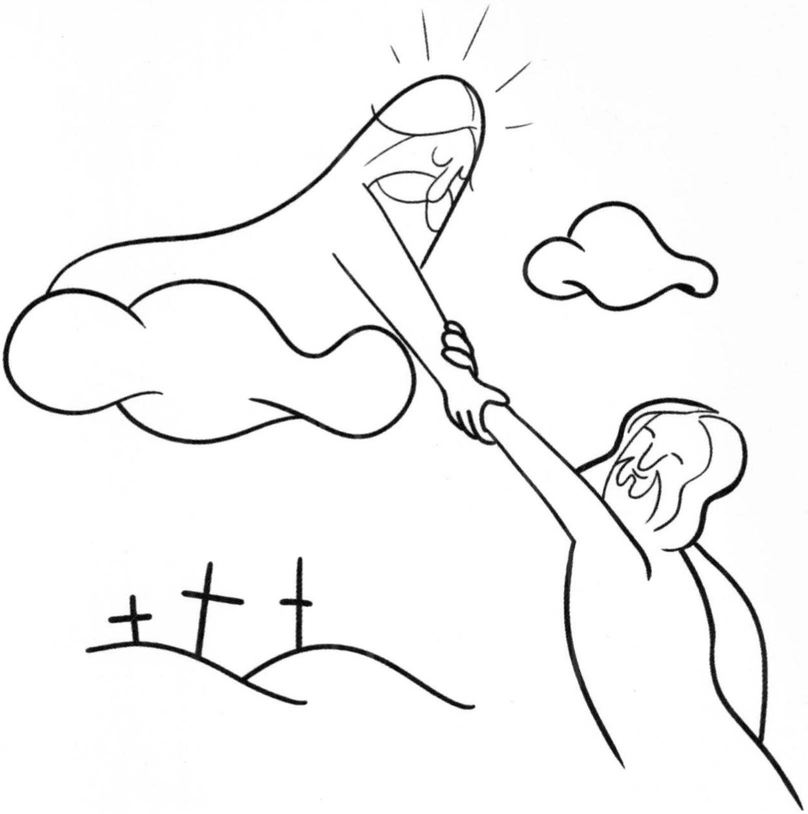

- Do you think you can be a Christian without believing in the resurrection of Jesus?

See also questions 14, 15, 19, 22, 27.

QUESTION 21

Where is Jesus now?

The last books of the Bible* describe the Ascension* of Jesus*, 'Jesus was lifted up before their eyes; a cloud hid him from view' (Acts 1:9). Christians believe that the resurrected Jesus had been present among the people in a special way for a while. With the Ascension of Jesus this mode of presence comes to an end.

The Ascension does not mean that Jesus took the elevator and went through the atmosphere, towards heaven. It symbolically makes clear that the risen Jesus is once again fully united with God* the Father*, from whom he originally came.

Does this mean that God – and more specifically Jesus – has abandoned or forsaken humanity? On the contrary. Shortly after Ascension, Pentecost* takes place. Then, in turn, the Holy Spirit* comes from heaven* to the world. He follows Jesus, as it were. With the difference that Jesus, the human, could not be everywhere at once, while God's Spirit – also called Helper – can be so. Thus the believers are now assured of God's constant help and assistance.

Catholic* Christians also believe that Jesus is present in a special way in the Sacraments* and in the living community of faith that they call Church*.

- Experiencing the presence of Jesus, what does this mean for you?

- Do you at times experience something that can be described as the presence of the Spirit of God?

See also questions 23, 25, 26, 28, 49.

QUESTION 22

What is the meaning of Jesus for people today?

The life of Jesus* has changed everything for mankind but at the same time nothing. God* has remained God and the human is still human. Yet Jesus makes everything different. He makes clear something that has always been there, but that has become completely visible through his life.

Christians believe that by living like Jesus, they can live fully themselves, beyond the threshold of death. The resurrection* of Jesus means that ordinary people can also rise. What is possible for one person – Jesus – is also possible for another. The first name Christians gave themselves was 'people of the road'. That way is Jesus. He is the way to perfect happiness and eternal life*.

This explains why Christians are people of hope. Not a naive hope, but a realistic hope. Hope that believes that a loving life – that does not run away from suffering and that strives for a better world – is definitive and therefore indelible. You can discover what true love is by looking at the example of Jesus every day. His life story is the inexhaustible textbook for becoming more and more human.

This does not apply to supermen, but to ordinary people. 'I have come to give people eternal life' (Jn 10:10), says Jesus. That eternal

life is not primarily the reward for our personal efforts, however important they may be. It's a gift you get when you open up to God's love. You would be grateful to God and Jesus for less.

- Does Jesus have a place in your life?

- Do you think there is a connection between faith in Jesus and hope?

See also questions 11, 12, 13, 20, 21.

QUESTION 23

Does the priest change the bread into the body of Jesus during Mass?

For Catholic* Christians, Communion* is the high point of Mass. They believe that they do not just eat a piece of bread or drink some wine. They believe that Jesus himself is present in a special way in that bread and in that wine and also in themselves when they eat and drink from it. This goes back to the last time Jesus sat at the table with his friends. He then said that the bread and wine he shared with them were his body and his blood. He then invited his friends to repeat this gesture. That is why Catholic Christians celebrate the Eucharist* (Mass) so often. In this way they remember again and again, and make real, that Jesus wants to give himself completely to the people.

This special presence does not mean that if a piece of bread falls to the ground during the Mass and you accidentally step on it, you trample Jesus. Catholic Christians treat the Eucharist with respect and keep the remaining hosts with great respect in a special place, called the tabernacle. For they believe that the living Jesus is present in the host in a unique and special way.

This touches on something typical of the Catholic faith: the belief that the risen Jesus was not only active long ago, but is also active today in the world and in the Church.

- Have you ever been personally touched by the celebration of the Eucharist or the Holy Communion?

- Do you see God at work in our world, here and now?

See also questions 3, 11, 17, 21, 22.

QUESTION 24

Is God a judge who condemns?

Christians believe that God* will ultimately judge everyone's life. This is what Christians call the final judgment*. Are Christians therefore afraid of a strict God who judges and thus also condemns?

You need not fear a God who is love. The only criterion that God uses to judge, is that of love. God looks straight into the heart of every human being, without ever making a mistake. He does not look for the bad things there. God only gauges how much that heart, during a person's life, opened itself up to love. Not even the smallest spark of love escapes God's attention. It is that experience of love that survives death.

God can only assess what has in fact happened. So it matters what a person has or has not done in life. Christians believe that they are free and therefore responsible for their actions, both good and bad.

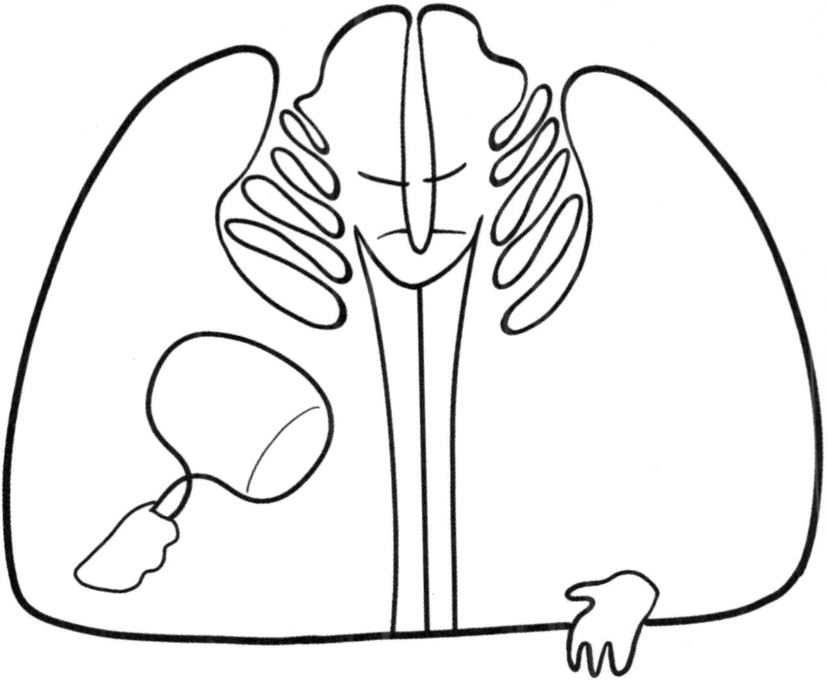

- Are you afraid of God?

- When you look at people around you, do you mainly look at the good, or do you focus on the bad?

See also questions 10, 34, 37, 38, 41.

QUESTION 25

Who is the Holy Spirit?

Christians believe that God* is Father*, Son and Holy Spirit*. Most people can imagine the Father and the Son but not the Holy Spirit? How can you imagine that? What is special is that the Holy Spirit, unlike the Father and the Son, does not speak anywhere in the Bible*. The Spirit has something inexpressible. Of the three divine persons, the Holy Spirit is by far the most mysterious.

In the Bible, the Spirit is also called fire, breath or wind. The Holy Spirit exists and lives in the heart of God and of Jesus*, as the fire of divine love. Fire that is and passes on heat and light. For the Spirit does not remain hidden in the heart of God, the Spirit comes out. The Holy Spirit gives God's love to people. In this way the Spirit brings people into contact with God and Jesus and opens them more and more to them.

So the Spirit is the passing on of love, the love that exists between the Father and the Son, but also the love of Father and Son for people. That is why Christians believe that the Spirit unites and desires to unite all in the one love that is God and is mentioned as the third. In a mysterious way the Holy Spirit completes the love-work of God. Like the wind, of which you do not know in advance where it is blowing.

- Can you imagine the Holy Spirit?

- Does the Holy Spirit have a place in your life of faith?

See also questions 7, 16, 21, 26, 27.

QUESTION 26

Do Christians believe in one God or in three gods?

Christians believe in Jesus*. They call him 'Son of God'*. Jesus, the Son, teaches who God the Father* is. In turn, the Holy Spirit* makes it possible to believe in the Father and the Son. But do Christians believe in one God or in three gods?

Christians believe in one God, just like Jews* and Muslims. What is specific about Christians – and different from Jews and Muslims – is that they believe that in the one divine nature there are three persons: God is three-one. How is this possible? Isn't this a contradiction? God is Father, Son and Spirit at the same time. Each of the three divine persons is completely God and at the same time completely different from the others. Just like every human being is completely human and yet unique, with the difference that there is only one God and many people.

The Bible* does not explicitly speak about the Trinity. Yet from the story of creation* on you see traces of diversity in the one God. God is love. So he cannot be lonely. In him there is diversity and connectedness. God-Father gives life to God-Son. God-Son receives the life of God-Father and entrusts himself entirely to him. Love is giving and receiving. Love is exchange. God-Spirit is the love that exists between Father and Son.

Can you really understand the Trinity? Augustine (354–430 CE) is known for his vast learning. While writing a book about the Trinity he once walked along the beach. There he saw a child pouring seawater into a hole with a shell. Augustine asked the child what he was doing and he answered that he wanted to pour the sea into that hole. Of course that is not possible. Then Augustine understood why his work of writing was so difficult. Understanding the Trinity is as impossible as what that child was trying to do.

- Do you relate to Augustine or do you find the Trinity easy to understand?

- Does faith in the Trinity help you to better understand the mystery of God?

See also questions 2, 9, 10, 15, 25.

QUESTION 27

When did Christianity begin?

Christianity* only really started after the death of the cross and the resurrection* of Jesus*. Not when Mary* became pregnant or on Christmas*, when she gave birth to her baby. Not even at the time when Jesus chose twelve collaborators and later placed Peter* at their head. Everything indicated that the enthusiastic movement that arose around Jesus had been completely shattered by his terrible death. His followers chose to hide. Everything seemed to have failed.

No one had expected or dared to hope for Jesus' resurrection. It is, right up to today, seen by Christians as God's confirmation that Jesus was right. The resurrection proves that his life is not a tragic failure. In no way did God abandon Jesus, quite the contrary. The new encounters between the disciples and the risen Jesus form the beginning of the Church*.

Of course, the time that Jesus travelled around with his disciples was very important for the emergence of Christianity. His words and deeds from that period teach us a lot about him and about God. Death on the cross proved that he wanted to give his life for his message of love and hope, but it was only through the resurrection that this became really clear.

However, the Christian faith only came out of the starting blocks after Pentecost*. Then the first followers of Jesus received the Holy Spirit*. The first testimonies show that there was still a lot of fear among the first Christians. They preferred to keep their message indoors. At a certain moment this fear turned into faithful trust and enthusiasm. From that moment on, the first Christians came out to share the Good News of Jesus with everyone.

- What do you consider to be the foundations of your faith?

- Have there been times of crisis in your life of faith?

See also questions 18, 19, 20, 25, 28.

QUESTION 28

Can you be a Christian on your own?

There is a saying, 'A lonely Christian is a dead Christian'. It is difficult, almost impossible to be a Christian on your own. You need others. Does this mean that Christians are wimps with insufficient backbone to believe independently? It has nothing to do with that. Experience shows that Christians are sometimes exceptionally brave. Some people are not afraid to risk their lives for their faith.

But being a Christian is more than a pastime or hobby. Faith is something that you receive, pass on, celebrate and experience together with others in the Church*. Jesus* says, 'Where two or three believers are together, so am I' (Mt 18:20). The Christian faith is an adventure that has been going on for 2000 years, with billions of participants. It is so broad and deep that it is impossible for one person to explore it alone. You need signposts so you don't get lost, and especially fellow believers to whom you can turn when you are discouraged or when you feel lonely.

The Church is the community that brings people together and gets to know Jesus. The Church has been doing this from the beginning. The Church proclaims the Gospel* and tries to help believers find the right path.

Some have a hard time with the Church. They see little connection between real Christian life and the rigidity of the institution. This is understandable. After all, the Church is not only a human community, but also a centuries-old, complex organisation. In addition, the Church has made mistakes and continues to do so. Yet the Church is often called 'mother'. As imperfect as the Church is, it passes on faith in Jesus. That is why many people love the Church. They are grateful to it because it has given them the faith, the most beautiful thing they have.

- Are there people you can turn to when you have questions about your faith?

- What do you think is the strength of the Church? What do you think is the Church's main weakness?

See also questions 27, 29, 31, 33, 39.

QUESTION 29

Why is there a pope?

The Catholic* Church* is like a ship that has been on the move for 2000 years. That ship has about 1.3 billion people on board, spread all over the world. A ship like that could use a good helmsman. This is the pope*, the bishop* of Rome. He is the successor of Peter* who, at the time, Jesus* appointed as the first of the apostles*. Peter's tomb is in Rome. This is why Rome has gradually become the centre of the Catholic Church.

The pope's task is to ensure that the Church remains one. He also makes sure that the faith that Jesus himself gave to the people is passed on faithfully from one generation to the next. He does all this together with the other bishops. Sometimes one or another point of Jesus' message is not in fashion. However, the Church is not a democracy in which a majority can vote to abolish or change such a point. The Catholic Church has a hierarchical structure, with the pope as the person ultimately responsible. Together with the other bishops he leads the Catholic believers.

Some beliefs belong to the unchangeable core of the faith. Other aspects are more a matter of interpretation or adaptation to culture, and therefore are changeable. The distinction is not always easy. It is the task of the pope to make the final decision. This may lead to personal unpopularity, especially with some who are wrong. That is why it is sometimes said laughingly that there is only one thing worse than a pope: no pope! Then you are up a creek without a paddle!

❧ How do you deal with points of faith that are difficult for you?

❧ Do you think it's a good thing that there's a pope?

See also questions 11, 27, 28, 30, 48.

QUESTION 30

Could the pope be mistaken?

In the Catholic* Church* you sometimes hear about the infallibility of the pope*. This can make eyebrows arch. Does this mean that Catholic Christians believe that the pope can never be mistaken? Of course not. Everyone can make a mistake, including the pope. Only God* is never mistaken. Nevertheless, Catholic Christians believe that there are exceptional circumstances in which the pope speaks infallibly about a point of faith.

The conditions for this are strict. It must be about the core of the Christian faith, as it can be found in the Bible* and the faith of the early Christians. In addition, the pope must speak on behalf of the whole Church and with the Church's consent. Finally, he must make it clear that he chooses to speak with this exceptional authority.

Over the past 150 years, there has been one statement by a pope that is considered infallible: the one about the Assumption of Mary*, in 1950.

Belief in the infallibility of the pope means, first and foremost, that Catholic Christians trust that God will help his Church in a very special way to deepen their faith in Jesus*.

- Has someone ever helped to strengthen your faith?

- Who or what helps you to deepen your knowledge of your faith?

See also questions 4, 27, 29, 42, 44.

QUESTION 31

What is the difference between an ordinary person and a saint?

In the Bible*, holiness* or sanctity is the quality of God* par excellence. God is holy. In the beginning of the Bible it is written that God created people in such a way that 'they resemble him' (Gn 1:27). That is why it is logical that this holiness of God radiates into the lives of those who are inspired by God. That is why in the first centuries of Christianity* it was customary for the priest* to address the faithful during the celebration as 'you, the saints'.

Christians are still inspired by God. So hopefully they continue to reflect something of God's holiness today. For most of them this is done in an inconspicuous way, but for some it catches the eye. That is why it is customary in the Catholic* Church*, after a long and thorough examination, to officially canonise some deceased Christians. However, most of the saints are and remain unknown, except to God.

Catholic Christians consider these saints to be great treasures: these men, women and children are valuable examples on whom you can model yourself in confidence for your own life. On the outside, their actions often seem quite normal, but at the same time they show that a life like Jesus'* brings out the most beautiful things in people. So much so that you recognise some of the beauty of God in it.

- Who are the most beautiful people you know?

- Do these people teach you something about God or about Jesus?

See also questions 15, 16, 24, 25, 32.

QUESTION 32

Do Christians believe in Mary?

Christians* worship God*, Father, Son and Holy Spirit. They do not worship Mary* but in their prayers ask her to pray with them to God. Nevertheless, it can be said that Mary is the most important woman in Christianity*. What is so special about her?

Mary is the mother of Jesus*, who Catholic, Orthodox and some Protestant Christians believe is the Son of God. That is why Catholic, Orthodox and some Protestant Christians say about her that she is the mother of God. But Mary is not a goddess. She is a human being, a unique person. That is why many Christians honour her in a special way. You can say that Mary was such an exceptional person because she could open herself one hundred per cent to God. So much so that she could receive him as a mother in her womb. Catholic* Christians therefore believe that Mary has never committed sin*. In other words, she has never, in any way, distanced herself from God. In that sense she is an example to all Christians. Believers can be inspired by her to become more faithful people in their turn.

Catholic Christians also ask Mary for her help. Because she is so intensely connected with God and with Jesus, she can help them to get closer to God and Jesus through her prayer.

– Is there something in the life of Mary that particularly appeals to you?

– Completely, or more and more open to God: what does that mean for you?

See also questions 15, 16, 22, 31, 45.

QUESTION 33

Is everyone a sinner?

For Christians, the word 'sin'* always says something about their relationship with God*, especially about how that relationship is challenging them to live a fuller life. Sin is actually about saying 'no' to God's invitation to live fully. It is about refusing the outstretched hand, because of, for example, anxiety, anger, stubbornness or sadness. As a result a person becomes isolated, instead of blossoming into openness and joy.

Sin can be about what you do or don't do, and what you think, say, and so on. You can sin against God, but also against yourself or against other people. To know if something is sinful, it is not enough to look at the outside. Often it is necessary to know with what intentions you do or don't do something. A well-known example is that of giving alms to a beggar. That always seems good, but you can also give money to someone to make that person dependent on you.

Sin can be about serious things, but also about small, seemingly unimportant things. These peccadillos can be more harmful than heavy sins, because they are repeated more often. Many little ones make one big one.

Sin can only exist if you both realise that an act or attitude is harmful and you agree to it in freedom*. Without consciousness and freedom there is no responsibility and therefore no sin.

Sin is something that all people have to deal with, even if they often don't want it. The Bible* expresses this in this way: 'I don't do the good I want to do, but I do the evil I don't want to do' (Rom 7:19). Christians believe that Jesus* has not sinned.

- What does sin mean to you?

- Do you relate to what the Bible says about not wanting to do sin but still doing it?

See also questions 14, 24, 34, 35, 41.

QUESTION 34

Does God forgive all sins?

Christianity* is the religion of love and therefore of forgiveness. That is why Christians believe that it is God's desire to forgive all sins*. In the Gospels* Jesus* constantly forgives sins. When he hangs dying on the cross, he even asks his Father* to forgive his own murderers.

God doesn't forgive because people deserve it or are entitled to it but just out of love, just like that. Yet God's forgiveness is not the same as putting your dirty laundry in the washing machine. It is not automatic. God is always willing to forgive, but you must accept that forgiveness. This is not as easy as it seems. Experience shows that there are a number of conditions for this.

First, it is necessary to acknowledge that you have sinned. You show that you repent. One of the signs of this is your willingness to do things differently from now on. Also, if possible, to make up for what you did wrong. If, for example, you have stolen, it is important to return the stolen goods or to repair the damage in some other way. This proves that you are actually repentant.

In the Catholic* Church* this reconciliation with God can be experienced in a special way. Believers can express their sins in a confidential confession* with a priest*. In such a conversation it is

important to actually mention your sins. But even more important is that the priest may then, in God's name, pronounce forgiveness. The most important condition for this is that those who ask God for forgiveness want to repent.

- Do you think forgiveness is important?

- Do you believe that there are things that should not or cannot be forgiven?

See also questions 24, 33, 35, 38, 49.

QUESTION 35

Why should you forgive?

Jesus* asks you to forgive those who have wronged you, and more than a little bit. He asks to forgive 'seventy times seven times' (Mt 18:22). But is forgiveness possible? And if it is at all possible, is it desirable? Isn't forgiveness for the weak? Isn't revenge more powerful?

Forgiveness is not cowardly, on the contrary it requires that you dare to face up to the evil that the other person has done to you. That's why forgiveness can hurt, but forgiveness is above all liberating. Not only for those who are forgiven but especially for the victim who can forgive. Forgiveness means that you can finally let go of anger, resentment and other negative feelings. Without forgiveness, these feelings threaten to grow deeper and take up more and more space. This is why forgiveness fosters inner healing, makes new life possible and gives hope. Forgiveness means that you can really turn the page on any evil in your life.

Forgiveness becomes easier when the perpetrator regrets and asks for forgiveness. But fortunately, the victim is not a hostage to the goodwill of the perpetrator. You can also forgive if the perpetrator is unknown, has already died, or does not repent at all. You don't need the offender's permission to cut the chain of the feelings of revenge.

Christians believe that in the end it is God* who forgives, through them. That's why they find it useful to ask God in prayer to be able to forgive. Even if you want to sometimes, you can't just decide to forgive. Forgiveness of those who have done you harm is given to you. Suddenly you can feel that the time is ripe. That's why Christians call forgiveness a grace*. It is a gift from God.

- Do you find forgiveness difficult?

- Are there things that make it easier for you to forgive?

See also questions 14, 22, 38, 46, 49.

QUESTION 36

Is purgatory a punishment?

For Christians, the prospect of eternal life* is a source of hope, but sometimes it can seem a little too easy. People are all too aware of the fact that not everything in their lives has been for the best, that, more often than they like, they flew out of control and did things that they are not proud of. Does the transition to eternal life mean that all that negativity disappears like snow in the sun?

After centuries of praying* and thinking about this question, Catholic* Christians gradually grew to believe that there is such a thing as purgatory*. This is not so much a place. It is rather a state of transition between life here on earth and eternal life. It is not a punishment, but a period of mourning. It is a necessary experience of purification to fully open up the gateway to God's love in heaven*.

You could compare it to breaking your leg. After removing the cast, you don't immediately walk around freely and easily. You need to practice with your stiff leg first. This is not easy, but you know it makes you better. It's like stepping out of the shade into the full sunlight, your eyes need time to get used to it. The same goes for purgatory.

- What helps you to feel 'pure' again when you have spun out of control?
- If you forgive someone yourself or are yourself forgiven by someone else, is that possible immediately or does it take time?

See also questions 33, 34, 37, 38, 41.

QUESTION 37

What do humans do in heaven?

There are no eyewitness accounts of life in heaven*. Yet the Bible* and the Christian experience of faith teach a lot about life after death. Words can only express the content of this in a poor way. Christians believe that human beings are made to live forever, rather than to disappear into the abyss of death. That, after death, you will forever be with God*. That is why Christians believe that in the hereafter there is no place for suffering and violence but only for love and joy.

What will you do there? Eat rice porridge with a golden spoon? The recipe book of heaven is unfortunately not known. We do know, however, that in the Bible eternal life* is often compared to a festive meal: a pleasant encounter where people celebrate together. You could say that you are already building our future eternal life, day in, day out: if you really love people, are good to others, share beautiful things with others, are close to others, open up yourself to God in silence. That can never be taken away from you again. That is just like eternal life.

In other words, real life, real love and real beauty are never lost. All the divine things that happen to you during your life, no matter how short or unseen, are eternal. Although a human life on the outside sometimes seems to be one big failure, God's gentleness keeps tracking down that authenticity. Life and love, no matter how modest, open a person forever to God, who is the source of it and who desires to share it forever with God's beloved people. In this sense, eternal life has already begun.

❧ Do you have any vision of what heaven will look like?

❧ Do you believe that you will go to heaven later?

See also questions 14, 19, 21, 22, 36.

QUESTION 38

Does God want evil?

Evil is perhaps the most important reason why people cannot believe in a good God*. If God wanted evil, then God could not be a good God. If God did not want it, then apparently God cannot prevent evil, but then God is not really God. Reason alone cannot explain it. Does this mean that the Christian faith has nothing to say about the difficult question of evil? Certainly not. The life of Jesus* shows how a person can ultimately be freed from evil.

Christians believe that God has become a human person. In other words: God does not live at a safe distance from evil. Jesus did not escape from evil. God has chosen to expose himself to evil. In this way, the suffering of ordinary people has also become the suffering of God. Indeed, Jesus, the Son of God, has suffered in the most horrible way the destructive effects of evil. He was even killed by it.

At first sight, therefore, it seems that evil has destroyed Jesus, but those who know the whole story know that Jesus has overcome evil through the love with which he answered it. Jesus' resurrection from the dead is the confirmation of this.

Is this an answer to the question 'does God want evil'? It shows that, in the confrontation with evil, God does not abandon people. Together with them God takes up the fight. However strong the

evil may be, Christians believe that God's love has overcome evil.

- Is there a connection between God and evil for you?
- Do evil and suffering make it more difficult for you to believe in God?

See also questions 15, 18, 19, 20, 39.

QUESTION 39

Does suffering make sense?

Christians believe that there is nothing good about suffering in itself. God* doesn't want it. Suffering makes no sense. Therefore it is not good to consciously seek it out. Suffering must be fought.

No one escapes suffering, not even Jesus*. In his life he suffered much. Christians are inspired by his example to endure the suffering in their lives as well as they can. What can you learn from this in concrete terms?

Jesus does not comply with suffering. He doesn't suggest refined theories about it either. He fights it, with word and deed. Jesus gives bread to the hungry and defends those who are threatened with death. When he is powerless in the face of the suffering of friends who mourn for a dead man, he tries to share that suffering. Compassion relieves pain.

The most intense experience of Jesus' suffering is his death on the cross. He did not want to die of torture. Jesus could have escaped that extreme suffering. He deliberately didn't do that. By this choice, Jesus did not justify the suffering. His death on the cross is the place where Jesus finally and completely showed that love is stronger than anything, even stronger than death.

In turn, Christians are invited to take up their cross. To love, like Jesus, only to love over and over again, even when it hurts. Some Christians go very far into following this example of Jesus. They accept the risk of being robbed of their lives because of their faith in God's love. They are called martyrs*.

- Can you learn something from the way Jesus dealt with suffering?

- Taking up your own cross, does that mean anything to you?

See also questions 14, 18, 20, 22, 27.

QUESTION 40

Does the devil exist?

It is sometimes said that it is the devil's* greatest victory when he can make people believe that he does not exist. The devil has already lost that battle. He seems to be back again. Christians believe that the devil is more than a myth or a symbol, even though he is not a person. Everyone has experienced that the power of evil exists, whether you call it devil, Satan, enemy, evil or otherwise.

The devil, Christians believe, is not the god of evil who can compete with the God* of Jesus*. He is not a rival to God. However ugly he may be, he is already defeated and not equal to the power of God's love. That is why it is not good to give him too much attention.

All the devil can do is divide and destroy. He is also exceptionally wise. He often says the right things. He does this not to build up but to destroy. That's why it's not good to enter into a dialogue with him, especially at night, when your thinking skills are at a low level.

Often the devil works by telling people seemingly pleasant things. That's why he is sometimes called the tempter or the seducer. However, the devil is in the detail.

When you take up his proposals, it always ends badly. If you have

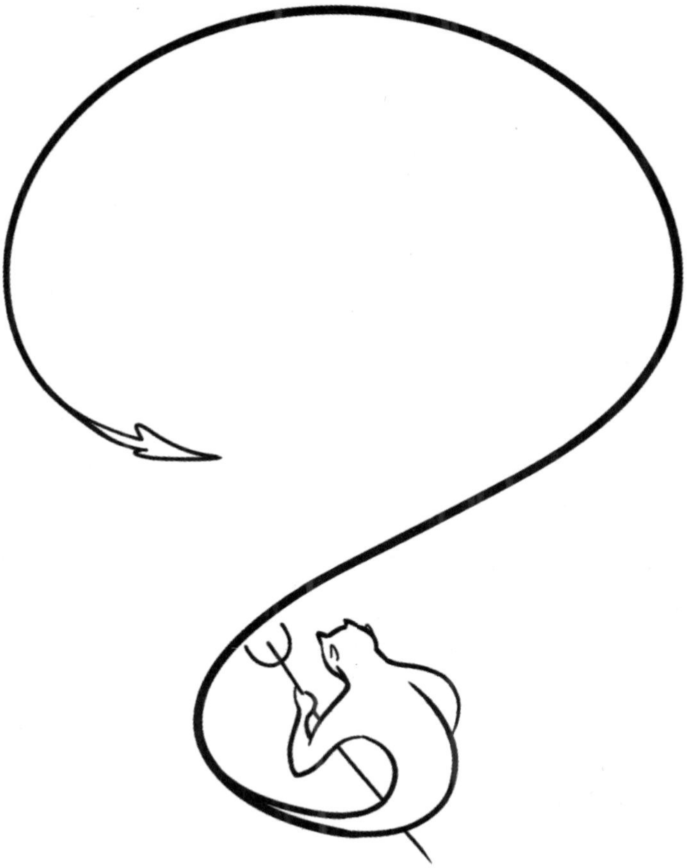

the impression that you are being attacked by devilish thoughts, it may be good to talk about it with a wise person in whom you have faith. The devil prefers to work in secret. When his secret plans come to light, he runs away.

- How would you describe the devil?

- Do you experience the attraction of evil?

See also questions 33, 34, 36, 38, 41.

QUESTION 41

Does hell exist?

The word 'hell'* has a nasty connotation. Hell refers to eternal pain and despair, as a punishment for what a person did wrong in their life. In ancient paintings about hell you can see how people burn alive in glowing oil, chased by scary devils. You would be afraid of less. But can Christians believe that? God* is love, isn't he? Isn't God always ready to forgive? How can a righteous God punish some people forever so terribly?

These are legitimate objections. Yet Jesus* repeatedly speaks about hell. How can that be explained? Actually, the question of whether or not hell exists is not about God's love, but about the freedom* of the human being, and thus about human responsibility. Christians believe that a person is free and therefore also responsible for their actions. A person can choose to do good or to give in to evil. The people who completely and consciously choose evil go to hell. Hell is the result of the voluntary, complete refusal of everything that God is and wants. It is the complete absence of any experience of love. Human freedom means that you are free to turn against God and that God respects your freedom.

So yes, hell exists, but not so much as a physical place as a possible state. You can ask whether someone is in this state, or if there are people who have never received or given a single flash of love in their whole life. It is possible that hell is empty.

- What do you mean by hell?

- Have you ever experienced, heard or seen anything that you would describe as hell?

See also questions 14, 34, 36, 38, 40.

QUESTION 42

Is the Bible dictated by God?

Christians like to call the contents of the Bible* the 'Word of God'. They believe that God speaks as it were in the many books that make up the Bible. So Christians believe that the Bible is inspired by God in a unique way. If you want to know the God of Christians better, there is no more reliable scripture imaginable. Yet the Bible is not literally dictated by God, as you can record a message on your smartphone.

Scholars have shown that it took more than a thousand years to write the complete Bible. Numerous people in all sorts of places were involved. What's special is that only a small part of the texts that have been written by the faithful during all those centuries eventually ended up in the Bible. For example, there were dozens of different gospel books in circulation among the first Christians. Only four of them have been selected: those of which the Christian community gradually began to see that they told the story of Jesus* in the purest and most correct way.

Conversely, you have a book like the Song of Songs that did end up in the Bible. The Song of Songs was originally written as a wedding song. In that short booklet there is no explicit mention of God, just because it is not about him. The Song of Songs poetically describes the experience of the loving desire between man and woman, but

in such a way that the believers gradually read it as an image of God's love for people and of people for God. This is how a non-believing book ended up in the Bible.

- Is the Bible for you a book like any other or does it have something special?

- Are there characters or stories from the Bible that you love especially?

See also questions 7, 29, 43, 44, 50.

QUESTION 43

Did everything in the Bible really happen?

The Bible*, Christians believe, is the Word of God*. So it contains no lies. That does not mean, however, that you can take everything in it literally. The Bible contains many different kinds of texts: myths, letters, law books, poems, more or less precise descriptions of historical events, visions, teachings, among others. Therefore, you cannot read all these different texts in the same way. Just like you would read and interpret a news item differently than you would a poem today. Yet you do not say that a poem is a lie.

Thus the story of creation at the beginning of the Bible is not meant as a scientific description of the origin of the world and humanity. Rather, it is a symbolic and poetic expression of the belief that the world was not created by chance but by God's love. So this is not so much a description of what happened, as it is an attempt to represent its meaning.

The sometimes very detailed stories about the passion and the crucifixion* of Jesus* or about the apparitions of the risen Jesus, have a more historical character. Archaeological research shows that this also applies to a number of other texts from the

Bible. Many facts from these bible stories are confirmed by the excavations in the Middle East.

- Do you find it difficult to know what you can or cannot take literally in the Bible?

- What helps you to better understand the Bible?

See also questions 2, 4, 8, 42, 44.

QUESTION 44

Can you be a Christian without knowing the Bible?

For Christians the Bible* is the most important source of knowledge about God* in general and about Jesus* in particular. Christians all over the world read and study the Bible. Many also pray* daily with texts from the Bible. It is an endless source of information about how God, for thousands of years, has made himself known to men and women. Thus you can consider the four Gospels* as exclusive eyewitness accounts of people who knew Jesus up close. There are no other books where you can learn more about him.

However, there are people who rarely or never read the Bible and yet are Christians in heart and soul. The reason is simple. Christians do not believe in a book but in a person: Jesus. In the end it is all about Christians living with Jesus and like Jesus. The connection with him is the most important thing for the life of a Christian. No matter how unique and irreplaceable the Bible is, a person can also get to know Jesus through other ways, such as prayers, testimonies of Christians or celebrations in the church*.

- Is the Bible important to your faith?

- Who or what feeds your faith day in and day out?

See also questions 7, 11, 14, 42, 43.

QUESTION 45

Prayer, what is that?

For the Christian, prayer* is about a relationship with God*, and in particular with Jesus*. It is your deepest self opening up to God. It is to listen to him in his presence. To pray is to be loved by him and to speak to him in confidence. In prayer, all masks can be removed. God can only come in to you when you are willing to be known as you are. One time you will be happy, the next you will be sad. It is possible that you are angry, with God or with a person. You may also express anger in your prayer.

Prayer is not inborn. It is something you can learn. Luckily you don't have to invent it all by yourself. Christians have been praying for two thousand years. So a lot of know-how has been developed. If you are looking for what can help you to pray yourself, it is good to let yourself be inspired by that.

There are as many different ways of praying as there are people. Some people like to pray with texts, whether or not from the Bible*. Others like to pray without words. You can pray alone or with others. You can pray in a quiet, secluded place or in the middle of the hustle and bustle of the city. Some like to pray for a long time, for others, the shorter the better. A good way of praying is a way that, at that moment, helps you to live more connected with God. This can change over time. What helps you get to God today may not work as well tomorrow. This is not strange. That's how it is for most of a person's life.

- Is prayer important to you?

- If you pray, how do you do it?

See also questions 7, 11, 46, 48, 49.

QUESTION 46

Is prayer useful?

The question of the usefulness of prayer* is often asked. However, this is not a good question. Prayer is not useful in the sense that it would make you smarter or richer. You can compare prayer with just spending time with a friend. No matter how good and important this is for the friendship, it does not provide any measurable added value.

Christians do believe that prayer is meaningful. Prayer changes a person because in it you are brought closer to the core of life. Opening yourself to God* helps to distinguish the important from the incidental. It sharpens the gaze and widens the heart. Prayer gives strength and courage. The Gospels* tell us that Jesus* often prayed. Sometimes all night long.

Many people love to pray with gospel stories. By praying and listening to Jesus, you can get to know him better, love him more and be more like him. It brings you closer to God and can make you a better man or woman.

In the Gospel, Jesus invites people several times to ask God in prayer for everything that is close to their heart. 'If you ask something, you will get it' (Lk 11:9) Jesus himself says. This is sometimes called a prayer of petition. But experience teaches that

God is not a Saint Nicholas (or Santa Claus) who serves at your beck and call. Often God's answer to your questions will be very different from what is expected or hoped for – he has something better in store for you. Christians indeed believe that God knows people better than they know themselves. That is why God knows better what a person really needs. This makes prayer an exercise in letting go of your own answers and trusting in what God wants to offer you.

➺ Has prayer ever changed something in your life?

➺ What makes a prayer meaningful to you?

See also questions 7, 11, 24, 45, 47.

QUESTION 47

Does God have a plan for everyone?

Christians believe that God* calls each person in a unique way. That calling* is about how you can best shape your life. Not that God has a compelling master plan for everyone. There is room for a personal, creative interpretation of that invitation. Like everything else in a person's life, that vocation and the answer to it can develop further during life.

If you listen attentively to your heart, you can track down your vocation. By learning to discern what gives you deepest joy. For Christians believe that God created them for joy. That is why coming closer to God is usually accompanied by feelings of peace and confidence, usually not in a spectacular way, but strong enough to withstand inner storms. For even when you have found your vocation, these will still appear now and then.

You can ask whether a person is still free when God calls them in this way. Christians believe that learning to accept that divine invitation is the culmination of freedom. After all, it means that you hold less and less on to things that do not belong to the core of life. You learn to leave those wrong tracks behind you to choose a life in which you as a human being really develop yourself.

Does this only apply to Christians? No, God loves all people equally, whether they are Christians or not, but Christians do have a great advantage. Their faith allows them to be inspired over and over again by Jesus*, the one of whom they believe that he is such a perfect person that he is God at the same time.

- Do you believe that you have a vocation of your own?

- If so, how did you find out?

See also questions 6, 14, 15, 46, 48.

QUESTION 48

Why are there such great differences between individual Christians?

There is a kind of basic belief that all Christians have in common. This goes back to the Bible*, to ancient texts such as the creed* and to the practices of the first generations of Christians. At the same time, there are big differences in the way people experience their faith day in and day out. This also applies to Christians of the same Church*. These differences can be so great that one sometimes wonders if these people believe the same thing.

The reason is simple. There is no computer program for Christian faith that guarantees an identical religious experience for everyone after uploading. The Christian faith is not a set of rules and regulations that you have to follow exactly. The core of the Christian faith is the personal relationship between a person and God*, especially with Jesus*.

A relationship lives and develops. Because every believer is different, every personal relationship with God and Jesus also has its own emphases. These have a lot to do with one's personality and life story. For some, the experience of the goodness of God is in the foreground. Another person will find inspiration in the humility

and simplicity of Jesus. For yet another, Jesus' commitment to a better world will be particularly important. These personal points of attention can evolve by what a person experiences or simply by age.

This diversity is not a problem. It is a richness. The Christian faith is so infinitely broad and deep that you cannot welcome everything in your soul at the same time, even if you might want to. It is all the believers together, the community of the Church, who have the fullness of faith.

- Are there things in your life that you would describe as typically Christian?

- What do you think is important in your faith and how does it develop?

See also questions 6, 11, 29, 45, 47.

QUESTION 49

Is being a Christian above all a matter of doing your best?

If you read in the Bible*, you will quickly come to a shocking discovery. You will notice that God* loves people very much and gives them new opportunities time and time again. The people in the Bible, for their part, are constantly getting it wrong. They answer God's love and faithfulness often with betrayal and infidelity, even though they would often want it to be different. In the life of Jesus*, people's refusal to do what God asks of them culminates when they kill him. All of Jesus' good friends are fleeing. The news of the resurrection* is received with unbelief. Each time Jesus takes the first step and gives new confidence and new opportunities.

In short, people want to choose the good, but on their own strength they can hardly do so, no matter how much they desire it. Certainly, it is not easy to be a Christian today, but, in fact, it has never been easy.

Is being a true Christian impossible? Certainly not. There is a good reason for this. Christians do not only believe that God is completely present in Jesus. They also believe that to this day God wants to live in every person, literally as in a house. And that he wants to give each person the strength to live well. This explains why it is that Christians often feel powerless and helpless with what the Gospel* asks of them. And that, at the same time, they ultimately turn out to be able to do much more than they had thought, often to their own surprise. Christians call that constant help from God his grace*.

Do you think it is possible to really live like Jesus?

God's grace, does that mean anything in your life?

See also questions 6, 14, 22, 33, 35.

QUESTION 50

Can Christians learn from other religions?

In the Gospel*, Jesus* says of himself, 'I am the way, the truth, and the life' (Jn 14:6). Jesus does not say a way, a truth or a life. This is no coincidence. Christians believe that Jesus teaches people fully and definitively who God* is. That's why Christians consider him unique, incomparable with anyone or anything else. This does not mean that Christians believe that non-Christian religions are wrong in all respects.

As early as the second century of our era, there were Christian scholars who believed that there are valuable, albeit incomplete, access routes to God in other religions as well. They call them 'seeds of the Word'.

In the centuries that followed, this openness was considerably overshadowed. In the second half of the twentieth century there was a radical turnaround. At that time, the Catholic* Church* explicitly called for respect, dialogue and cooperation with the other religions. As far as Islam and even more so Judaism are concerned, it was emphasised that there is a great deal in common, even if there are major differences.

It is therefore safe to say that Christians can indeed learn from

other religions. This applies in particular to the way in which others experience their faith. It is sometimes said, for example, that Christians can learn from the powerful hope of the Jews and from the fervour of Muslims' faith. Jews and Muslims, in turn, could learn from Jesus how to love more inclusively.

- Are you positive or suspicious of other religions?

- Have you ever learned anything from other religions that has enriched your own faith?

See also questions 11, 14, 22, 26, 42.

QUESTION 51

Can a Christian believe in reincarnation?

The reincarnation faith comes from India. It says that a person can be born several times, each time in a different body. In the Far East, reincarnation is considered as bad news: it is still not done, you have to start over again before you are freed from your body. In the West, people look at it more optimistically. They see it as a new opportunity after a failure. This Western variant appeals to quite a few people.

For several reasons, Christian faith and reincarnation cannot be combined. Christians believe that you only have one life. This gives you a special responsibility. What you do or don't do is important and irreversible. This is different if you have multiple lives. If it doesn't work now, it's not so bad. Better luck next time.

Moreover, the Christian faith attaches great importance to the unique personality of each person. It is so valuable that it is mysteriously preserved after the resurrection*, in the afterlife. Reincarnation, on the other hand, assumes that the challenge lies in letting go of one's own personality and merging into the great, divine whole.

The view of the body is also different. For Christians, the body is so important that they believe it will rise, even though the body that has risen will be very different from the mortal body. For people do not only have a body, each person is a body. Body and soul are one, inseparable whole. Reincarnation ultimately considers the body worthless. You have to become a pure spirit and free yourself from your body as quickly as possible.

Christians believe that the resurrection is a gift that God* offers just out of love. Reincarnation is about merit.

- Does it seem attractive to you to be reborn?

- Do you think having your own personality is important or would you rather get away from yourself and merge into a greater whole?

See also questions 14, 19, 20, 22, 49.

QUESTION 52

Has Jesus laughed?

It can't be *proved* that Jesus* laughed. In many images Jesus looks severe or sad. The Bible* explicitly mentions that Jesus cried, and that he was sometimes angry but never that he laughed.

Usually religion is associated with deep and serious things. Could this really not go hand in hand with laughter? Jesus also says in the Bible, 'I want you to feel the same joy as I do. I want your joy to be perfect' (Jn 15:11). Indeed, there is a lot of evidence that Jesus loved to laugh and laughed a lot.

Jesus was a real man. He did what ordinary people do. He was not a teetotaler. Jesus loved to dine and enjoyed good wine at weddings. He preferred to do this together with others. Some of his opponents even accused him of being a party animal. We know that Jesus was a born storyteller. People were hanging on his words. Jesus loved the birds and the flowers. Above all, he loved other people, like no other person has ever loved other people.

In short, Jesus showed all the qualities of a happy and joyful person. So Jesus also loved to laugh well. There is no other way.

- What is the connotation of the Christian faith for you: serious, sad, joyful?

- Are there aspects of the life of Jesus and of the Christian faith that make you happy?

See also questions 7, 13, 14, 15, 47.

52 Words

1. ANGEL

Angel literally means 'sent one'. The Bible often mentions angels. They are messengers of God who, in the name of God, share something with people. Often when God comes to people in the Bible, this is done by means of an angel.

2. APOSTLE

At the beginning of his mission, Jesus chose twelve collaborators. They are called apostles. It was their task, together with Jesus, to proclaim the Gospel to the people. Catholic and Orthodox Christians consider bishops to be the successors of the apostles.

3. APPARITION STORY

At the end of the Gospels there are stories of the apparitions. They tell how the friends of Jesus met him after his death. Before that they had already seen that his grave was empty. These meetings have contributed a lot to the belief in the resurrection of Jesus. They have in common that the friends had a hard time believing this.

4. ASCENSION

The Gospels describe Jesus' ascension as the end of his physical presence on earth. It takes place forty days after his resurrection. Since his ascension, Jesus, the Son of God, has returned to God the Father, in heaven.

5. BIBLE

The Bible is a collection of books that Christians believe are inspired by God. By reading the Bible you can better understand who God is and more specifically who Jesus is. The oldest parts were written more than 3000 years ago. The more recent books are more than 1900 years old.

6. BISHOP

A bishop is a successor to the apostles. In the Catholic Church he is appointed by the pope. He is ultimately responsible for the faith of a local Christian community.

7. CATHOLIC

A Catholic is a Christian who is a member of the Catholic Church. Catholic Christians recognise the authority of the pope, the bishop of Rome. They attach great importance to the sacraments.

8. CHRIST

Jesus is usually called Jesus Christ in full. Christ means: the one who is anointed by God. The anointed one was and is the one who the Jews expect as the saviour sent by God. Christians believe that Jesus is that long-awaited Christ. Another widely used word for Christ is Messiah.

9. CHRISTIANITY

Christianity is a religion that originated from the person and the life of Jesus Christ, as described in the Bible. Christians believe that Jesus is the Son of the One God and that he has a special message for all people. Christianity originated from the Jewish* religion.

10. CHRISTMAS

Christmas is the feast of the birth of Jesus Christ. Christians commemorate God becomming human on that day, born in a child. It falls on 25 December. Christmas is preceded by a preparation time of four weeks, called Advent.

11. CHURCH

The word 'Church' has two meanings. When it means the building in which Christians come together to celebrate their faith it is written with a small 'c'. Church also means the large community of Christians – called the People of God – with its own organisation and habits. In that case it is written with a capital 'c'.

12. COMMUNION

Communion literally means 'community'. Catholic Christians refer to the special communion with God and with the other believers that arises during the celebration of the Sacrament of the Eucharist, when the believers eat the bread and drink the wine.

13. CONFESSION

Confession is one of the seven sacraments of the Catholic Church. It is also called the 'Sacrament of Reconciliation'. Confession means that you go to a priest to express the sins you regret. In the name of God, the priest can then forgive those sins. He will ask the penitent to correct the mistakes they have confessed to.

14. CREATION

Christians believe that God is at the origin of what exists, of creation. God continues to create, even today. If he would stop creating, then everything that exists would immediately cease to exist. God only creates out of love. God wants to share life with humanity.

15. CREED

A creed is a text that offers a compact summary of the Christian faith. The most important one was approved at a meeting of bishops in Nicea in the year 325 CE. All Christians have this creed in common.

16. CRUCIFIXION

Jesus was executed by crucifixion at the beginning of the thirties of our era (30 CE). The cross was then a tool of torture. Because the death of Jesus was followed by his resurrection, the cross has become the sign of God's love for Christians: a love that does not shrink from the worst violence and that is stronger than death.

17. DEVIL

The devil is a mysterious force that wants to bring humanity down. He stands for evil and sin. The devil is not on an equal footing with God and Jesus. He can do a lot of damage. Yet Christians believe that the love of God is stronger.

18. EASTER

Easter is the most important feast for Christians. It is the commemoration of the resurrection of Jesus, the third day after his death. Easter is preceded by the forty-day period, Lent, in which Christians give special attention to fasting, prayer and solidarity. Fifty days later, they celebrate Pentecost.

19. ETERNAL LIFE

Christians believe that people are made to live forever, in connection with God and each other. This eternal life is a state of complete and everlasting joy. To the extent that humanity already experiences this connection on earth, eternal life already begins now. Death, then, is not the end of human existence.

20. EUCHARIST

The Eucharist is one of the seven sacraments of the Catholic Church. It is the commemoration of the last meal Jesus had with his apostles, and more broadly of his death on the cross and resurrection. Catholic Christians – and some Protestants – believe that in every Eucharist Jesus gives himself completely to the faithful in the form of bread and wine. Eucharist is also called 'Mass'.

21. FATHER

Christians believe that God is Father, just as he is Son and Holy Spirit. This is not a statement about the gender of God. It does refer to hGod's active love. God is the Father of his Son, Jesus, and Father of all people to whom God constantly and gratuitously gives life. Just like Jesus, Christians believe that they can trust themselves to their divine Father.

22. FREEDOM

Christians believe in the freedom of the human person. The future is not written in the stars. That freedom is not complete. Yet, through that freedom, a person can make choices and give direction to his life. The completely free person is the person who can live completely according to the calling that God gives them, without getting lost on the wrong tracks.

23. GOD

Christians believe in one God. They believe who God is has become completely clear through the life of Jesus. He shows that the one God consists of three persons: Father, Son and Holy Spirit. All three are God. Together they form the triune God.

24. GOSPEL

Gospel literally means 'Good news'. It is the message of Jesus. In the Bible you can read it in four slightly different versions: by the authors Matthew, Mark, Luke and John. Each of these books is also called a Gospel. They are testimonies of faith, not objective reports of events.

25. GRACE

Christians believe that God offers his life and strength over and over again to the people who are open to it. This grace of God makes people capable of a lot, because it gives strength, inspiration and courage. God gives his grace just like that, without asking for anything in return.

26. HEAVEN

Heaven is the dwelling place of God. Christians hope and believe that, after their life on earth, they will go to heaven to live forever. What awaits them there is an endless experience of love and happiness, together with many other people and in connection with God.

27. HELL

Jesus speaks several times about hell. Hell is not a place. It is the condition of one who has consciously completely turned away from the love that is God. Hell is about loneliness, emptiness, meaninglessness and frustration, typical of a life separated from God. It is the opposite of the experience of fullness of life and love in heaven.

28. HOLY

Holiness or sanctity is the quality par excellence of God. The life of Jesus, man and God at the same time, shows that holiness is also accessible to human beings. In the Catholic Church there is a practice of declaring people holy or saint: people who radiate so much the goodness and beauty of God that they are set as an example for all believers.

29. HOLY SPIRIT

Christians believe in one God, and in that one God there are three persons: Father, Son and Holy Spirit. The Holy Spirit is God here and now, who comes into the human heart and makes it possible to receive the love of the Father and the Son. The Holy Spirit is often portrayed as a dove coming down from heaven.

30. HOST

Host is the name of the small pieces of bread that Catholic Christians use to celebrate the Eucharist. Hosts are usually round and made of unleavened wheat bread.

31. JESUS

Jesus was born in Israel around the year zero, in the Jewish family of Joseph and Mary. Around his thirtieth birthday he began to proclaim the Gospel. He was sentenced to death by crucifixion. Shortly after, the faith in his resurrection arose. Christians believe that Jesus is both man and God. That is why they call him Son of God. Together with the Father and the Holy Spirit he forms the triune God.

32. JEWS

The Jews are a people with their own religion, Judaism. The Jewish people come from Palestine, and is more than 3000 years old. Their holy book is the Bible, but without those parts that are about Jesus. Jesus was a Jew. The Christians consider the Jews as their older brothers and sisters.

33. JOSEPH

Joseph was the husband of Mary, the mother of Jesus. He was a carpenter in Nazareth, the village where Jesus grew up.

34. LAST JUDGMENT

Christians believe that God will judge people at the end of time. It is a judgment because everything will come to light, the good and the evil. It is also a promise. After all, God will then light up even the slightest spark of goodness or beauty of everyone, no matter how bad their life.

35. MARTYR

A martyr is a person who believes so much in Jesus and in God that, even if threatened with death, does not recoil. Many Christians, men, women and children, have been killed because of their faith. This still happens today.

36. MARY

Mary was the mother of Jesus. She was married to Joseph. As mother of Jesus, the Son of God, she is also called 'mother of God'. Christians believe that, after Jesus, she was the person who was most open to God. Christians believe that Mary was a virgin: 'she was found to be with child from the Holy Spirit' (Mt 1:18).

37. MIRACLE

A miracle is a special event that evokes amazement and in which the believer sees a sign of God's active love for people. For Christians, the resurrection of Jesus is the greatest miracle.

38. NEW TESTAMENT

The New Testament is the second and last part of the Christian Bible. It contains the writings about the life of Jesus, the way of life of the early Church and the teaching of his apostles. The first part of the Bible is called the Old Testament.

39. OLD TESTAMENT

The Old Testament is the first part of the Christian Bible. It contains the scriptures from the Bible that were written before Jesus. The second and last part is called the New Testament. There are small differences in the composition of the Old Testament between Catholic, Orthodox and Protestant Christians.

40. ORTHODOX CHRISTIANS

The Eastern Orthodox and the Catholic Church separated in 1054. The reason for this was a disagreement about how exactly to understand the trinity of God. Most Orthodox Christians live in Central and Eastern Europe.

41. PAUL

Paul was a very dynamic Christian in the early days of the Church. First he persecuted the Christians. However, Paul himself converted to the Christian faith and became one of the most important proclaimers of the Gospel. He travelled all over the Mediterranean. Some of the letters he wrote are included in the Bible.

42. PENTECOST

The feast of Pentecost is celebrated fifty days after Easter. On Pentecost, Christians commemorate the reception of the Holy Spirit after Jesus' ascension. The love and power of the Holy Spirit make the final start of the Church possible. The activity of the Holy Spirit continues to this day.

43. PETER

Peter was one of the apostles of Jesus. He was married. Catholic Christians believe that Jesus gave Peter the task of leading the early Church. He was the first bishop of Rome.

44. POPE

The pope is the bishop of Rome. Therefore he is the head of the Catholic Church. He is the successor of the apostle Peter, whose tomb is in Rome. He is elected by the cardinals. These are bishops who are appointed by the pope as his closest advisors.

45. PRAYER

Prayer is opening yourself up to God with your whole person. It is coming to God to listen to God, to speak or just to be present. There are many different forms of prayer: in silence, with words, singing, alone or in a group, short or long, in a church, at home or in nature. Prayer is often called the oxygen of the Christian faith.

46. PRIEST

Within the Catholic Church, the priesthood is a lifelong task. It can only be given to unmarried men through ordination by a bishop. It is the priest's task to proclaim the Gospel and to administer the sacraments. The priesthood itself is a sacrament.

47. PROTESTANT

Protestants are Christians. The break between Protestant Christians and the Catholic Church took place in the sixteenth century, during the Reformation. For Protestant Christians, the Bible is very important. They attach less importance to the sacraments than Catholic Christians and do not recognise the authority of the pope.

48. PURGATORY

Purgatory is a state of transition between the death of a person and eternal life with God. Catholic Christians believe that most people need an experience of purification after their death. Only then are they ready to be fully united with God's love.

49. RESURRECTION

Christians believe that Jesus really died on the cross and that God made him alive again and forever. This is the resurrection of Jesus. It is a sign of God's faithfulness to Jesus. It proves that the path of love leads to eternal life. Christians believe that all people will eventually rise and live on.

50. SACRAMENT

In the Catholic Church there are seven sacraments: baptism, confirmation, Eucharist, reconciliation or confession, anointing of the sick, priestly ordination and marriage. These are visible signs by which God grants his invisible grace to people. Catholic Christians believe that thanks to the sacraments, Jesus remains present among the faithful.

51. SIN

Sin is what a person does or does not do, and thinks or says, by which they go against God's will. In concrete terms, this means, somehow, refusing to really live and love. Sin can only be said to exist when a person acts consciously and in freedom.

52. VOCATION

Christians believe that God calls each person in a unique way, inspired by the example of Jesus, to give form and content to one's life. Living according to your vocation is the best way to your personal happiness. Marriage and becoming a priest are examples of vocation. Finding your vocation requires discernment.

Epilogue

This book focuses on the faith of the Christian faith community, not on the personal conviction of the author. This book is written from a Catholic perspective and with attention to the other Christian Churches.

I did not strive for completeness, either at the level of the whole, or at the level of the individual answers. The order of the questions is inspired by the Nicene Creed. Ethical issues are not dealt with.

The selection of themes is the result of numerous discussions with young people. I would like to thank Heleen, Jules, Marie and Melanie especially for this. Thanks also to Guido Attema, Karin Benoist, Sim D'Hertefelt, Matthias Kramm SJ, Jos Moons SJ, Katrien Sollie and Hans van Leeuwen SJ for their suggestions and comments. A special word of thanks, finally, to Rick Timmermans for sharpening the style of writing and to Paris Selinas for the drawings.

In writing this book I have consulted many sources. In particular, use was made of:

- *Book of the Faith of the Bishops of Belgium*, Lannoo, Tielt, 1987
- *I believe. An invitation to the 21st century*, Bernard Sesboüé SJ, Averbode, 2000
- *Catechism of the Catholic Church*, 1995, Licap - SRKK, Brussel, Utrecht, 1995
- *Youcat, the official youth catechism*, Lannoo, Tielt, 2011